TRIBES
of NATIVE
AMERICA

Seminole

edited by Marla Felkins Ryan
and Linda Schmittroth

**BLACKBIRCH®
PRESS**

THOMSON

™

GALE

121564

San Diego • Detroit • New York • San Francisco • Cleveland
New Haven, Conn. • Waterville, Maine • London • Munich

For more information, contact
The Gale Group, Inc.
27500 Drake Rd.
Farmington Hills, MI 48331-3535
Or you can visit our Internet site at http://www.gale.com

LIBRARY OF CONGRESS CATALOGING-IN-PUBLICATION DATA

Seminole / Marla Felkins Ryan, book editor ; Linda Schmittroth, book editor.
    v. cm. — (Tribes of Native America)
Includes bibliographical references and index.
Contents: Seminole name — Origins and group affiliations — Creek wars — Seminoles in Oklahoma — Religion — Government — Daily life — Customs — Current tribal issues.
  ISBN 1-56711-630-2 (alk. paper)
  1. Seminole Indians—Juvenile literature. [1. Seminole Indians. 2. Indians of North America—Southern States.] I. Ryan, Marla Felkins. II. Schmittroth, Linda. III. Series.
  E99.S28 S45 2003
  975.9004'973—dc21
                                                              2002008672

Printed in United States
10 9 8 7 6 5 4 3 2 1

Table of Contents

SEMINOLE

Name

The name Seminole (pronounced *SEH-muh-nole*) may be from the Spanish word *cimmarrón,* which means "wild one." It may also come from the Creek word for "runaway" or "lover of the wild."

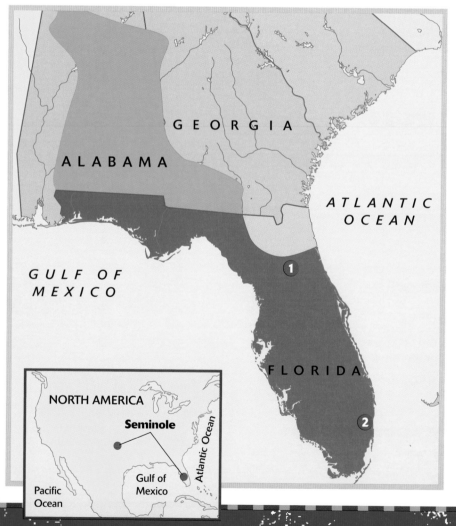

Seminole Contemporary Communities

Florida
1. Oklewaha Band of Seminole Indians
2. Hollywood Reservation Headquarters of the Seminole Nation of Florida, which includes: Big Cypress Reservation, Brighton Reservation, Immokalee Reservation, Tampa Reservation

Oklahoma
(Not on map; the Oklahoma Seminole live in 14 different towns.)

Light shaded area: Traditional lands of the Seminole before their move to Florida.

Dark shaded area: Homelands of the Seminole after the early 1700s.

Where are the traditional Seminole lands?

The Seminole people first lived in Alabama and Georgia. They moved to Florida in the seventeenth century to escape American colonists and traders. Today, there are six Seminole reservations in Florida. Seminole also live in 14 towns in Oklahoma.

Seminole children

What has happened to the population?

In 1821, there were about 5,000 Seminole. In a 1990 population count by the U.S. Bureau of the Census, 15,564 people said they were Seminole.

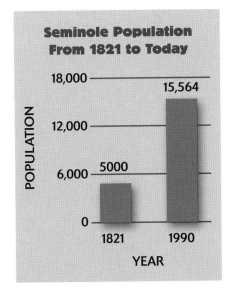

Seminole Population From 1821 to Today

POPULATION

18,000

15,564

12,000

6,000

5000

0

1821   1990

YEAR

Origins and group ties

Seminole was a name given to a group of Creek, Yamasee, Oconee, Apalachicolas, Alabamas, and other Indians who fled from Alabama and Georgia and went to Florida in the 1700s.

The Seminole did not exist as a tribe until the late 1700s. At that time, a group of Creek moved to northern Florida. This core group was joined by other tribes, as well as runaway slaves, and became the Seminole.

Seminole got around the swampy Everglades in wooden canoes, poling with long poles that have spears attached for catching fish.

Some Seminole reservation lands in Florida are near the Big Cypress Swamp (pictured).

HISTORY

Move to Florida

The people who became the Seminole first lived in Georgia. They were part of clans (large groups of related families). In the 1700s, some moved to Florida to avoid conflicts with neighbors.

The War of 1812

Most of the eighteenth century was peaceful for the Seminole. They had good relations with Spanish troops in Florida. They hunted and gathered, and traded their goods at Spanish forts. The Seminole warmly accepted runaway slaves from American plantations farther north. This period of peace ended during the War of 1812 between the United States and Great Britain.

Creek Wars

During the war, some southeastern Indians sided with Great Britain. Others supported the United States. In 1813, a group of Creek killed American soldiers at an army post near Mobile, Alabama. The army fought back. This led to the Creek Wars of 1813–1814. Many Indians died, and many of their towns were destroyed. The Indians had to sign a peace treaty. In it, they gave all their lands in

In 1813, Creek warriors attacked Fort Mims, outside Mobile, Alabama.

Georgia and some in Alabama to the U.S. government. Rather than be ruled by the U.S. government, many Creek fled to Florida and joined the Seminole. This tripled the Seminole population.

The First Seminole War

Large numbers of white settlers soon began to move southward. Fights between American settlers and the Seminole caused the United States to declare war on the tribe in 1817. This conflict was called the First Seminole War. American army troops invaded Florida in search of runaway slaves. This violated the boundary between the

1849
California Gold Rush begins

1861
American Civil War begins

1865
Civil War ends

1869
Transcontinential Railroad is completed

1917–1918
WWI fought in Europe

1929
Stock market crash begins the Great Depression

1932
Florida Seminole move to reservations

1941
Bombing at Pearl Harbor forces United States into WWII

1945
WWII ends

1950s
Reservations no longer controlled by federal government

1957
Seminole Tribe of Florida is set up and gains federal recognition

American soldiers captured Seminole chiefs during the First Seminole War.

United States and Spain, but Spain was too weak to fight back. As a result, U.S. raids increased, and American troops seized Florida. They burned native villages and killed the people. In 1821, Spain gave Florida to the United States. American settlers began to take over the best farmland and hunting grounds.

Move to reservations

In 1823, the U.S. government persuaded the Seminole to move to reservations in central and southern Florida. This would allow white settlers to take their lands. The tribe was promised equipment, livestock, and a yearly payment of $5,000 for 20 years. The Seminole gave up 30 million acres of rich farmland for about 5 million acres of sandy, marshy land not suited for farming. The Indians also agreed not to protect escaped slaves.

Move to Indian Territory

Over the next 10 years, many whites settled on former Seminole lands. When that land was filled, the whites wanted more. Government officials pressured Seminole leaders to sign the Treaty of Paynes Landing in 1832. The Seminole agreed to move to Indian Territory within three years. In return, they were promised cash and goods.

The Second Seminole War

The move to Indian Territory was supposed to take place in 1835. Before it began, Seminole chief Osceola started a rebellion that led to the Second Seminole War. Most of the tribe moved to Indian Territory, but nearly 500 members hid in the Everglades with Osceola. For seven years, the Seminole warriors resisted 5,000 U.S. soldiers. They struck at the troops,

The Second Seminole War began in 1835 and lasted for seven years.

Seminole chief Osceola was captured by U.S. troops in 1837.

then disappeared into the swamps. This conflict was the longest and costliest Indian war in U.S. history. Federal troops captured Osceola in 1837. He died soon after.

Osceola's successor, Chief Coacoochee, carried on the fight. He finally surrendered in 1841. By then, most warriors had been killed or had agreed to move west with the rest of the tribe. The Seminole became part of the movement of the "Five Civilized Tribes" to Indian Territory. The Five Civilized Tribes were the Chickasaw, Choctaw, Seminole, Creek, and Cherokee. Their white neighbors and the U.S. government gave them this name because they had adopted many white customs.

The Third Seminole War

Several hundred Seminole stayed hidden in the swampy Florida Everglades. For about 10 years, they were largely left alone. Then, in 1855, federal land surveyors trampled the cornfields and destroyed fruit trees at the home of Seminole chief Billy Bowlegs. An angry Seminole war party attacked the surveyors' camp and killed several of them. This set off the Third Seminole War (1855–1858). In 1858, the government offered the Seminole money to move to

Billy Bowlegs (left) led a group of Seminole to Indian Territory.

Indian Territory. Bowlegs and 123 men took the offer, but a few hundred others did not. Their descendants are now the Seminole people of Florida.

In Oklahoma

In Indian Territory, the Seminole faced many hardships. They were forced to live in harsh and unsanitary conditions with their former enemies. Many died. In 1856, the survivors got their own reservation.

The Seminole faced many hardships in Indian Territory—present-day Oklahoma.

White settlers complained that too much land was set aside for Indians. They also said that the Indians did not take on white ways quickly enough.

The government gave in to settlers' demands. To force the Indians to be more like whites, allotment laws began to be passed in 1887. Allotments split reservations into small parcels for individuals. Each Indian would tend his or her own allotment. The whole tribe could no longer tend a large plot, as was their custom. Leftover land was opened to white settlement.

The Seminole could not live off the land as they had done in Florida. Many had to sell their land to buy food and clothing. By 1920, four-fifths of their lands had either been sold or lost. The people scattered, and their culture suffered. Tribal self-government ended when Oklahoma became a state in 1906.

By 1920, four-fifths of Seminole land in Oklahoma had been bought or taken over by white settlers.

The people regrouped in the 1960s. They wrote a constitution and became the federally recognized Seminole Nation. In 1990, they received $40 million for lands taken from them in Florida.

A group of Florida Seminole pose in front of their village in 1910.

Move from the Everglades

The Florida Seminole were left alone for nearly 75 years after the Seminole Wars ended. The government tried to bribe them to move west, but the offers were ignored. Finally, in 1932, the Seminole agreed to move to land in central and southern Florida. Some became cattle herders. Others worked for wages. Today, the Seminole live on six reservations in Florida.

Religion

The Seminole saw no separation between body, mind, and soul. They believed in spiritual beings that dealt fairly with humans. One Seminole god was the Preserver of Life, who gave life and took it away. Another was the Corn Mother, the goddess of farming. Yet another was Thunder, the god of rain and war. In addition to good spirits, the Seminole believed that water panthers and horned rattlesnakes lived in the water and drowned swimmers. They also believed in little people who lived in forests.

Everyone in the tribe practiced everyday rituals to maintain nature's balance. People asked an animal's forgiveness before they killed it. Before they ate it, they tossed a piece of meat into the fire. This was a sacrifice to the slain animal.

Medicine bundles were sacred. They were made up of 600 to 700 bits of stone, herbs, dried animal parts, feathers, and other objects. They were used to protect the tribe's well-being.

The Seminole of Oklahoma call the "stomp dance" their traditional religion. The stomp dance comes from the Green Corn Dance, a ceremony the Seminole brought when they left Florida.

The Seminole of Oklahoma perform the "stomp dance" as part of their religion.

SEMINOLE POPULATION: 1990

The Seminole people of today live mainly in Florida and Oklahoma. The Seminole of Florida live on six reservations around that state, and the Oklahoma Seminole live mostly in Seminole County. In the 1990 U.S. Census, members of the various tribes identified themselves this way:

Tribe	Population
Florida Seminole	518
Oklahoma Seminole	450
Seminole	14,596
Total	15,564

SOURCE: "1990 census of population and housing. Subject summary tag file (SSTF) 13 (computer file): characteristics of American Indians by tribe and language." Washington, DC: U.S. Department of Commerce, Bureau of the Census, Data User Services Division, 1995.

Government

Each village and tribe had a government led by a chief. The chief made decisions on matters such as food storage, celebrations, building, and farm planning. The chief's position was sometimes inherited. Other times, though, he was chosen for his wisdom and experience. He had advisors and council elders to help him. A war chief took care of military matters. All people could give their opinions on major decisions.

Once they moved to the Everglades, the Seminole had to change their ways. The land was not good for farming, so women gathered plants while men fished and hunted. They were able to raise pigs and chickens in the hot climate.

The Seminole used canoes carved from tree trunks to travel the shallow waters of the Everglades. During the 1800s, they hunted deer, otters, raccoons, rabbits, turtles, alligators, fish, and birds. These animals were used for food and pelts. The Seminole exchanged pelts, alligator hides, dried fish, beeswax, and honey for European supplies such as coffee, tobacco, cloth, metal pots, knives, and liquor.

A Seminole man wrestles an alligator.

Between 1870 and 1914, Florida drained much of the Everglades. Some Seminole went to work for whites as hunters or fishermen. Although many still farm and raise cattle, they often need other jobs to support their families. Some sell arts and crafts, plant grass, work as loggers, or wrestle alligators. They also work in tribal bingo halls and casinos, their most profitable businesses. The Oklahoma Seminole have a bingo operation, a gaming center, and two trading posts.

DAILY LIFE

Families

Clans were named after animals. Children were born into their mother's clan. Families in the Everglades were usually made up of a husband and wife, their daughters and their husbands, children, and grandchildren.

In Seminole families, the men tilled the soil and the women planted and tended gardens. Everyone worked together at harvest time. Each family harvested its own share of food.

Buildings

Before the Seminole went to the Everglades, they often lived in villages of about 30 families. Each family used two buildings. They slept and cooked in the first one. The second was used for storage and to welcome guests. To build these structures, timber posts were sunk into the ground. Cypress or pine boards formed the walls.

Life in the damp, hot climate of the Everglades made new types of buildings necessary. The Seminole built open-sided huts called

The Seminole built open-sided huts called *chickees*.

Before they moved to the Everglades, the Seminole lived in villages similiar to this one.

chickees, with a raised floor and a roof made of palmetto leaves. The roof kept out rain, and a fire kept out mosquitoes. These structures were used only to sleep in and to store personal items. There was no furniture. Possessions were hung from the rafters. People slept on mats on the floor.

Clothing

Before they went to Florida, men wore loincloths (flaps of material that cover the front and back and hang from the waist). Women wore knee-length skirts. Garments were made from animal pelts or woven from plant fibers. In cooler weather, robes of fur or buckskin were draped over the shoulders. Children often went naked.

Men and boys wore loincloths.

Seminole men wear turban-like headdresses.

Fish was an important food for the Seminole.

Today, Seminole men wear turban-like headdresses. The women sculpt their hair into a rounded, slightly flat peak or roll above the forehead.

Food

In northern Florida, the Seminole planted corn, pumpkins, melons, squash, beans, and other vegetables. Men hunted and fished. Camps moved as the seasons changed to find wild fowl and game.

In the Everglades, the Seminole fished and hunted. The women gathered wild plants, palmetto, and cattail roots. They also collected roots called coontie that were pounded and made into flour. The people ate pineapples, oranges, and bananas. Palmetto berries were used to make molasses. In their limited garden space, they grew sweet potatoes, corn, pumpkins, sugarcane, and beans.

Education

Boys and girls learned from their parents and other elders. Mothers taught their daughters how to raise children, sew, and run a home. Boys learned how to

Seminole 23

ONE GROUP TRIES TO KEEP TRADITIONAL WAYS

A group of Seminole who call themselves the Independent Traditional Seminole lives about 30 miles northeast of Naples, Florida. They are not recognized by the federal government, and many other Seminole oppose them. The group, which numbers about 200, lives in the traditional way.

Some observers claim the Independent Traditional Seminole have adapted some parts of modern life, but in an unsafe way. One person saw electrical wires on the ground near the group's plywood chickees, and voiced fears that outhouses may contaminate groundwater. In the mid-1990s, the Collier County, Florida, government backed down from its attempts to make the people move out of their chickees or bring them up to county building codes. The Honor the Earth music tour raises money and awareness for ecological and native issues. In 1997, it focused attention on the Independent Traditional Seminole group. The tour supported the people's efforts to have a law passed to protect them from legal actions.

fish and hunt, and to make and use canoes. All children shared in the work of the village.

Children were told never to try to outdo another person. The culture still has this noncompetitive trait today. Children who misbehaved were punished with dry scratching. A wooden tool embedded with fish teeth or bone splinters was used to scratch the child lightly. This punishment caused more shame than injury.

Formal education did not begin until the 1920s, when some elementary schools were started. During the 1930s and 1940s, some children were sent to Indian boarding schools. There, they were forced to adopt white ways.

Today, children attend school on or off the reservation. Dropout rates are high. Since 1972, the tribe has worked to develop programs for pre-school children. It has tried to preserve Seminole language and customs. It has also worked to aid students who want to go to college. More young people now attend college and take jobs as doctors, lawyers, or engineers.

Seminole children still learn customs and traditions from their parents and elders.

Healing

The Seminole used herbs to cure illnesses. The most important one was red root, the inner bark of a type of willow tree. It could be soaked in cold water and used to stop nausea, fever, and swellings. A potion made of snakeroot or bear grass was pounded and mixed with water. It treated coughs, snakebites, and kidney troubles.

A Seminole medicine man performs a ceremony.

When herbs did not bring a cure, shamans (pronounced *SHAH-munz* or *SHAY-munz*) were called. They rubbed the patient's body, sang or said prayers, or made scratches on the skin just deep enough to make the patient bleed slightly. The Seminole thought a person's blood could be too heavy. This might cause illness or violence. Often, angry spirits were believed to cause illness. The shaman was asked to calm the spirit. Today, health care is available at clinics on or near the reservations.

Stitchery

Seminole women are known for their stitchery. They create patchwork designs to make colorful bands that are attached to skirts, shirts, and other items. Some designs are traditional. Others are unique creations of the seamstress. Each Seminole reservation is known for its own designs.

Seminole women are well known for their unique stitching designs.

Seminole women also make dolls from cloth-wrapped palmetto leaves stuffed with cotton. They dress the dolls in historically accurate clothing and hairstyles.

Oral literature

Seminole tales explain how the world was made and why certain rituals are performed. One story tells how a turtle rose from the sea to rest. His back started to crack, and people came out of the cracks. Then the cracks came together in squares. The people made their homes along them.

CUSTOMS

Festivals

Most Seminole ceremonies dealt with fire or water. Both were considered very sacred. The Green Corn Dance was one of the most important rituals. It is still performed by some natives.

Birth and names

Women gave birth at the baby house. This was a small structure used only for that purpose. The mother and newborn stayed there for four months. When the time had passed, the mother and new baby went home.

Seminole babies were placed in a cold stream right after birth. This was the first of many purification ceremonies they went through during their lives. Traditionally, names were given to Seminole infants by a tribal elder on the fourth day after birth. When they were 12, young men got new names at the Green Corn Ceremony to mark their maturity.

War rituals

To prepare for war, the men put red paint on their faces, necks, and chests. The Seminole were fierce

THE GREEN CORN DANCE

Corn planted in the early spring was ready to eat by early summer. The Green Corn Dance was held to celebrate the harvest. It was also a time to visit with friends and family, give thanks, and make up for past wrongs. Food was made from the past year's harvest and shared by all. Men and boys fasted and drank *asi* ("the black drink") to make themselves pure and powerful. They drank it until they vomited. They believed this gave them energy to dance all night long.

There were 40 corn dances. Both men and women took part in them. The men sang while the women kept the beat with tortoise shell rattles. Villages also played a fierce form of stickball. On the last day, all the cooking and hearth fires were put out and wood was set up for a new fire. Four perfect ears of corn were placed on the fire. Prayers were offered and a sacred fire was lit to burn the corn. This fire was used to rekindle all the others in the village. Then the men ate the fresh, green corn that the women had prepared. After the fire had completely burned the four ears of corn, and the men had had four rounds of asi, the ceremony ended. The New Year had begun.

warriors, but they were fair to their enemies. They spared the enemies' lives whenever possible. Captured enemies were made slaves, but could marry the women of the village. The children of these marriages became members of the tribe.

In traditional Seminole marriages, the wife was considered the head of the household.

Courtship and marriage

People had to marry someone outside their clan. A young woman was usually ready to marry at about age 14. At that time, she began to wear many beads and silver ornaments. Sometimes a girl's family chose her husband. Usually, when two people wanted to marry, they met with the leader of the woman's clan. They were then married, if there were no objections. Afterward, the married couple went to live with the bride's family for a few years, until they were able to start their own camp. The woman was considered the head of the household. The Seminole rarely divorced.

Funerals

Seminole burial places were in remote spots in the swamp or woods. All of a person's belongings were buried with him or her. It was believed that the tools would be needed in the afterlife.

Current tribal issues

Fierce independence, courage, and pride helped the Florida Seminole avoid the move to Indian Territory. They still show these traits today. They encourage their children to stay in school, work to improve health, and start new businesses. They are also involved in efforts to preserve the Everglades.

For the Oklahoma Seminole, it is important to keep their traditions. They also want to revive their stomping grounds (where ceremonies take place), and to raise educational and income levels.

Chief Osceola led warriors in the Second Seminole War.

Notable people

Chief Osceola (1804-1838) led warriors in a two-year campaign against the U.S. government. He fought until his capture in 1837, after which he died in prison.

Donald Fixico (1951-) is a professor of history and Native American studies. He has published many essays on Indian history, as well as a book on the effects of city living on Native Americans.

Betty Mae Tiger Jumper (1927-) was the first Seminole to earn a high school diploma. In the 1960s, she became the first woman elected as tribal chairperson.

For More Information

Brooks, Barbara. *The Seminole.* Vero Beach, FL: Rourke Publications, 1989.

Garbarino, Merwyn S. *The Seminole.* New York: Chelsea House, 1989.

Lee, Martin. *The Seminoles.* New York: Franklin Watts, 1989.

Official Homepage of the Seminole Nation of Oklahoma. http://www.cowboy.net/native/seminole/index.html

Sneve, Virginia Driving Hawk. *The Seminoles.* New York: Holiday House, 1994.

Glossary

Allotment a plot of land given to a person or group to cultivate

Bribe money or favor given or promised in order to influence the judgment or conduct of a person in a position of trust

Inherit to receive money or property from an ancestor

Plantation a large farm that usually has resident laborers

Purification a process done to make things clean, or free of imperfection

Successor one who comes after another

Surveyor a person who examines a situation and collects data

Treaty an agreement

Unsanitary not clean

Index